Feelings Do Matter

A Teen's Guide to Understanding Feelings

"Owl Letha" to the Rescue

Joyce G. Moore, Author

Scot Mmobuosi, Illustrator

Feelings Do Matter
A Teen's Guide to Understanding Feelings

By Joyce G. Moore

ISBN: 978-1-931259-15-6

For information contact:
Joyce G. Moore
Post Office Box 1683
Marietta, GA 30061

Printed in USA

Owl Letha says: "Wise up, because awareness is powerful"

Introduction

Inside and outside of every person there is a communication system of feelings. This network serves to reveal how we feel when certain things, events, people and/or situations affect us. This internal and external system is always aware of how our feelings have been altered. Sometimes we are unable to explain in detail but we can sense when something has changed.

We do become what we feel, because the way we feel affects our attitudes, our actions, our moods and our overall focus on how we tend to react. Our feelings affect our mental attitude concerning life. Sometimes others endeavor to tell us how we should feel. However, they do not know everything that has happened that affects how we have arrived at our feelings.

"Owl Letha" wants to help you to understand the many feelings that you may experience. "Owl Letha's" mission is to help identify some of these feelings and help you to have more happiness and peace in your daily life. It is important to spend more time in "The Comfortable Zones" and less time in "The Uncomfortable Zones".

Important Disclosure

The information contained in this publication is not intended to offer any conclusive diagnosis in regard to a person's feelings, emotions, actions and/or any other behavior.

A person should quickly seek professional help to clarify any condition that may feel unnatural or uncomfortable. The information is for educational purposes only.

Dedication

This publication is dedicated to all of our youth who are striving to achieve success in life. We must remain vigilant and provide solutions regarding teen violence, gun violence, the toxic involvement of social media, dating abuse, unwanted sexual encounters, bullying, shaming, 'ghosting', drug abuse and the rise of teen suicides. It is of utmost importance to recognize how hormonal changes during puberty affect emotions and behavior. There is a serious need to inform any affected segments of a population as to how to maintain awareness in all areas, in an effort to reverse the negative effects of so much trauma.

The hurtful behavior of others has a profound effect on our ability to live our lives in peace and harmony. Without proper wisdom and guidance, the task becomes very difficult and confusing. The informative content of "Feelings Do Matter" is designed to offer some needed insight into some of the ways that the readers can identify the various emotions in "The Uncomfortable Zones" and review some of the conducts to achieve the desirable feelings to remain in "The Comfortable Zones".

Think About It

1. We can have many different feelings at the same time and this can be very confusing. Being informed and having the ability to identify the underlining cause can help to minimize the confusion. The contents of this book are designed to be a guiding light for the reader.

2. We can't make others treat us with the love and respect that we feel that we deserve. However, we should always do the things that are required to love and respect ourselves. It is important to be your own best advocate and protector.

3. Bullying, 'name calling', disrespectful behavior and any forms of demeaning of another, are some of the ways that some may attempt to control another person. No person or animal ever deserves to be mistreated by anyone. Each person must continue to protect themselves and seek help if needed.

4. When feeling any undesirable emotions it is important to identify why you are feeling this way and quickly take appropriate actions to correct the situation that may be the cause. Many solutions may be contained in the following pages of this book.

5. Continue to be very aware of the people, the things, the events, the situations and other causes that may block you from being in your own "Comfort Zone". This zone is your safe space and you must protect it from any invasion or intruders.

6. What you think of yourself matters a lot. So, continue to practice doing the things for yourself that will help you to build and maintain self-confidence.

7. It is very important to continue to express gratitude and appreciation to those people who show up and support you. The list includes parents, family, friends, teachers, neighbors, school staff, community leaders and anyone who offers encouragement and those who extend other kind deeds.

8. The things that you do to your body and the things that you put in and on your body will affect you physically, mentally, emotionally and/or spiritually. Do not participate in the use of any illegal drugs, illegal substances, alcohol, watching violent 'entertainment' and/or any activities that may provoke adverse behavior.

9. It is a fact that everyone does not always practice respect for others. It is true that "Hurt people, hurt people". This does not mean that you have to ignore the behavior of those who are hurting and allow them to hurt you. Just be aware of those who are repeat offenders and the actions that you must take.

10. When you are sad others do not always feel your pain or understand the reasons that you appear sad. Open up to those who express concern and work to resolve your feelings. The content of this book is your special guide.

Content

Content

The Uncomfortable Zone of Sadness

Sadness is to be avoided at all costs. This emotion makes us feel unhappy and blocks our ability to feel joy and peace. Sadness may cause us to have feelings of being depressed, not being satisfied with life, not being understood and not having a special sense of purpose. Sadness must be replaced by joy and other feelings of life enhancing moods. It is important to take proper actions and move to "The Comfortable Zone of Joy" as quickly as possible.

Prepare to Move Forward

It is important to think of things, people, events, talents, activities and other ideas that will help bring needed joy. Sit in a quiet space and let your imagination work for you, as you prepare to move to "The Comfortable Zone of Joy".

The Comfortable Zone of Joy

In "The Comfortable Zone of Joy" you will feel a great sense of peace and happiness. You must strive for a natural feeling of contentment and satisfaction. As you seek an inner sense of purpose and meaning in your young life, you will realize that there is so much meaningful work to be done. Things do not happen automatically. You must set meaningful goals for yourself and continue to focus on achieving these goals and seeking help from those who really have your best interest in mind. As you learn to cope with the things that just don't feel right, but they are not in your control to change, you will release the sadness. "The Comfortable Zone of Joy" is your special place and you must continue to protect it from anyone and anything that may attempt to extinguish it.

Personal Pledge

I will maintain and protect my personal Joy by finding my purpose
and identify and avoid any issues that cause me sadness.

The Uncomfortable Zone of Hurt

Feelings of being "Hurt" may be from physical pain caused by some injury to your body or mental pain that was caused by something that someone said or did to cause emotional harm. Either distress may linger and affect your mood in many areas of your life. It is vital that you identify the cause of the "Hurt" and take proper action to minimize or eliminate the "Hurt" as quickly as possible. Identify who you may need to discuss your feelings with. Do what it takes to resolve the feelings. It is important to swiftly move to "The Comfortable Zone of Relief".

Prepare to Move Forward

It is important to think of things, people, events, talents, activities and other ideas that will help bring needed "Relief". Sit in a quiet space and let your imagination work for you, as you prepare to move to "The Comfortable Zone of Relief".

The Comfortable Zone of Relief

In " The Comfortable Zone of Relief" you are seeking to experience feelings of relaxation, peace, comfort, and dismiss any pressures that made you have feelings of discomfort. You can take back your power when you practice the art of forgiveness and letting go of any bitterness. This practice of forgiving anyone who has caused you to feel "Hurt" is to your advantage. You will now allow yourself to have a sense of letting go of emotional pain and moving on to better things and better thoughts. By holding on to any negative feelings you are only hurting yourself and that is not at all productive. "The Comfortable Zone of Relief" is yours to claim and it is up to you to forget the hurtful past and live in the peaceful present.

Personal Pledge

I shall exercise my power to forgive and reconcile,

by releasing any thoughts of any discomforts

to my mind, body and spirit.

The Uncomfortable Zone of Hate

Hate is a feeling of intense or passionate dislike for something or someone. This emotion is very dangerous because it brings about anger and aggressive hostilities. "Hate" may cause a person to physically cause harm to themselves and/or someone else. Hate may stem from fear, insecurity, mistrust, mistreatment, dislike, prejudice, misinformation and so many imaginary thoughts. Whatever the root cause, it is critical to move from "The Uncomfortable Zone of Hate" and move to "The Comfortable Zone of Empathy".

Prepare to Move Forward

It is important to think of things, people, events, talents, activities and other ideas that will help bring needed "Empathy". Sit in a quiet space and let your imagination work for you, as you prepare to move to "The Comfortable Zone of Empathy".

The Comfortable Zone of Empathy

In "The Zone of Empathy" you will allow yourself to seek an understanding of how much better it feels to be in a place where you are free from "Hate". It is vital to practice acceptance and eliminate any thoughts of dislike (imagined or real) regarding the situations surrounding the uncomfortable feelings of hate. If the emotion of hate is caused by an idea that someone does not act or behave as you would like, it is necessary to adjust your expectations and not attempt to "fix" another. The big question to ask yourself: Why should you continue to hurt yourself by staying in the "The Uncomfortable Zone of Hate"? Seek peace and embrace empathy. Practice acceptance and tolerance for the things and people who you cannot change. Change your attitude and position yourself to live a more peaceful life.

Personal Pledge

I shall embrace empathy.

I shall practice acceptance and tolerance for the things
and people who I cannot change and dismiss thoughts of hate.

The Uncomfortable Zone of Anger

Anger is an emotional feeling of displeasure with something and/or someone. During a period of anger a person becomes upset and may act out with rage and/or violent language. Anger flares up in instances when someone feels that they have been treated unjustly, have been physically injured, have experienced some personal loss, are in some physical pain, experience extreme boredom, frustration, feeling unfulfilled, feeling inferior, feeling left out or excluded, a biological disorder, and for an endless number of unknown and unexplained reasons. Whatever the cause, anger increases the risk of affecting the mental, physical, emotional, spiritual and/or financial health of an individual and of society. It is important to move to "The comfortable Zone of Affection".

Prepare to Move Forward

It is important to think of things, people, events, talents, activities and other ideas that will help bring needed "Affection". Sit in a quiet space and let your imagination work for you, as you prepare to move to "The Comfortable Zone of Affection".

The Comfortable Zone of Affection

In "The Zone of Affection" it is important to appreciate your own special personality and exercise needed control over your thoughts, feeling and actions. It is critical to dismiss any expectations of perfection in yourself and in others. When any feelings of anger arise, it is helpful to sit, close your eyes and take a series of deep breaths and allow yourself to simmer down. A safe space is your personal refuge and your "Comfort Zone" to avoid conflicts and instill affection for yourself. Focus on loving yourself too much to let any situation and/or person cause anger to flare up and control you. You must resolve the conflicts within your own inner-being. If there is a medical condition or too many reoccurring bouts of anger, it is vital to seek professional intervention as quickly as possible. There is no shame in seeking help.

See page 63 Triggers for Anger Rage and/or Antagonism

Personal Pledge

I shall seek my personal refuge and focus on affection and love for myself
and let peace and harmony be my calming thought.

8

The Uncomfortable Zone of Loneliness

Loneliness is an emotion that may flare up when a person is alone but they would rather be in the company of another and/or others. This is a state of mind where someone feels empty of social contact or they may even feel unwanted and/or unneeded. Some people require more social contact than others. Not everyone feels the need to be in social environments in order to avoid feeling lonely. Being alone can be a safe zone for people who enjoy solitude and being in their own creative space. So, everyone has a different need for human contacts. A pet can fill the need for companionship and provides for needed comfort. For those who have a need for human intervention to avoid feeling lonely, they may need to venture out and not remain in physical isolation. Loneliness can affect mental and/or physical well-being if it becomes uncomfortable for too long.

Prepare to Move Forward

It is important to think of things, people, events, talents, activities and other ideas that will help bring needed "Inclusion". Sit in a quiet space and let your imagination work for you, as you prepare to move to "The Comfortable Zone of Inclusion".

The Comfortable Zone of Inclusion

In "The Zone of Inclusion" a person becomes involved in activities that align with personal attitudes, talents, beliefs, interests and feelings of purpose and fulfillment. Within this zone it is a special time to meet a person or people who appeal to your sense of friendship and moral values. Observe the character of those in the environment and take time to evaluate their personal appeal. Determine if they have the personality of someone that you want to include in your inner circle and if you want to be included in theirs. Take time to "size others up" before "jumping to conclusions". The "Inclusion Zone" may change from time to time. Do not do anything against your moral character in order to be included. Always have "an exit strategy". Do not be forced to 'go along in order to get along', just to be included.

Personal Pledge

I shall always find ways to practice love for myself

by doing things that offer me personal joy.

(with or without being in the company of others)

(A good book, my special music, my creative imagination)

The Uncomfortable Zone of Weakness

Weaknesses may be felt physically, mentally, emotionally, spiritually and financially. It is a lack of strength or being inadequate or inefficient in some areas of a person's life. Any area that requires a person to become more competent is considered a zone of weakness. When a person desires to achieve something and they do not have the skills, the knowledge and the strength, this can cause disappointments and feelings of being unqualified and weak. They may feel like a failure and inferior to others. This is an "Uncomfortable Zone" to be in. Much work is needed to make the successful move into "The Comfortable Zone of Strength".

Prepare to Move Forward

It is important to think of things, people, events, talents, activities and other ideas that will help bring needed "Strength". Sit in a quiet space and let your imagination work for you, as you prepare to move to "The Comfortable Zone of Strength".

The Comfortable Zone of Strength

In "The Comfortable Zone of Strength" you will exercise your power to fortify your physical, mental, emotional, spiritual and financial well-being. Personal strength supports us in our abilities to achieve our personal goals. There are so many areas in our daily lives that require strength. We need muscle strength, a strong skill set, educational strength, fortitude, resourcefulness, flexibility, structure, initiative, wisdom, creativity, persistence, insight and strength to turn disappointments into opportunities to improve on our strength building. You can continue to stay in "The Comfortable Zone of Strength" when you continue to apply yourself and stay focused on your obligations to seize every opportunity to become informed about life skills and continue striving for independence.

Personal Pledge

I shall seize every opportunity to improve my strengths
in every area of my life and practice self-dependence.
(Physically, mentally, emotionally, spiritually and financially)

The Uncomfortable Zone of Unfulfillment

Unfulfillment can be uncomfortable because it causes a person to feel a sense of emptiness and dissatisfaction with the way that their life is progressing. There is a feeling of being "at a dead end" and no directions for moving ahead. Without the wisdom and the energy to move forward this can be emotionally draining. Some of the things that may cause a person to feel unfilled includes internalizing the criticisms of other and not feeling good enough, jealousy, envy, boredom and lack of available resources. It is critical to analyze the possible causes and quickly move to "The Comfortable Zone of Satisfaction".

Prepare to Move Forward

It is important to think of things, people, events, talents, activities and other ideas that will help bring needed "Satisfaction". Sit in a quiet space and let your imagination work for you, as you prepare to move to "The Comfortable Zone of Satisfaction".

The Comfortable Zone of Satisfaction

In "The Comfortable Zone of Satisfaction" you will have a sense of fulfillment as you experience contentment and serenity. It is important to identify the people, the situations, the tangible things and any desired achievements that are required to fulfill your needs. Once you identify these things, you must focus on the order of your priorities and work to get any needed assistance. Some things cannot be achieved alone. Consider the categories that you feel any sense of unfulfillment. Some examples: Family life, school environment, lack of purpose, employment, health, confidence, vision for the future, relationships, freedom, finances, etc. Continue to stay focused and extend gratitude to all who assist you in your "Comfortable Zone of Satisfaction". Celebrate accomplishments with expressions of gratitude.

Personal Pledge

I shall continue to focus on the positive actions that I must take

in order to live in my personal "Zone of Satisfaction"

and continue to seek needed assistance and offer heart-felt gratitude.

The Uncomfortable Zone of Rejection

Rejection includes feelings of being denied, excluded. eliminated, refused, etc. When a person feels any of these schemes of not being included, it can be emotionally hurtful. Feelings of rejection may cause sadness, anger, shame, resistance, loneliness, confusion, jealousy, abandonment, etc. Not knowing the core reason is unsettling. Even when discovering reasons that may be given, it may cause feelings of disbelief and shock. It is important that the rejected person reaches a point of acceptance, when decisions are beyond their ability to control and quickly move to "The Comfortable Zone of Support".

Prepare to Move Forward

It is important to think of things, people, events, talents, activities and other ideas that will help bring needed "Support". Sit in a quiet space and let your imagination work for you, as you prepare to move to "The Comfortable Zone of Support".

The Comfortable Zone of Support

In "The Comfortable Zone of Support" you will feel surrounded by people who will accept you and include you in their "Inner Circle". You will feel a peaceful sense of belonging. Any thoughts of being rejected or excluded will vanish. You will embrace being among those who offer a genuine sense of connection. You will come to realize that some things and some connections with certain people are not intended to be. You must realize that being rejected does not define you. Continue to process your emotions and learn how to move forward based on an honest reality of the situations and the people who you encounter. Refrain from forcing any relationships that are not in your best interest. If something is not meant to be, let it be and move on.

Personal Pledge

I shall continue to connect with the people who accept me for who I am
and I will not feel defeated by anyone who does not embrace me.

The Uncomfortable Zone of Confusion

Confusion is a mental state of being unclear, uncertain or being in a quandary. This state of mind can immobilize a person, keep them from moving forward and prevent them from making needed decisions. Without having critical information and clarity, being in the zone of confusion hinders progress. This dilemma may have an effect on an individual and/or many others. This lack of clarity can affect a person's sleep, their relationships and an endless number of other aspects of their lives. This is why it is critical to quickly move to "The Comfortable Zone of Clarity".

Prepare to Move Forward

It is important to think of things, people, events, talents, activities and other ideas that will help bring needed "Clarity". Sit in a quiet space and let your imagination work for you, as you prepare to move to "The Comfortable Zone of Clarity".

The Comfortable Zone of Clarity

In "The Comfortable Zone of Clarity" you will be able to see a clear path forward in any of the decisions that you must make. You will know how to gather information that is needed to make decisive moves and make wise use of your time and other resources. Seek a special private space and quiet your mind. Stillness allows you to be in a good mental state as you take time to review the issues that may be causing confusion. With a clear mind, issues will come into focus and you will be motivated to make the necessary decisions that will create space for you to be in a more peaceful and calming zone of clarity. Create the winning plan, claim it and keep it. Take advantage of connecting with nature and enjoying the natural surroundings on a clear day. Clear all of the negative thoughts and reenergize.

Personal Pledge

I shall work to quickly identify any issues that are causing me confusion
and quickly resolve my state of confusion by seeking clarity
with the help of those who are qualified to help me.

The Uncomfortable Zone of Shyness

Shyness can be a feeling of awkwardness and having low self-esteem. This can cause a person to react with apprehension and uncertainty. A shy person may find it painful and uncomfortable being around unfamiliar people. This emotion affects how they interact with others and may cause them to become withdrawn and fearful of connecting on a social level. This level of insecurity may cause depression and sadness. It may be difficult for the cause to be identified if the shy person is unable to reveal the areas of their personal discomfort. So, only the shy person can provide the information that is needed to help them to overcome their shyness. They must open up to a trusted professional and receive the needed help in order to move to "The Comfortable Zone of Confidence".

Prepare to Move Forward

It is important to think of things, people, events, talents, activities and other ideas that will help bring needed "Confidence". Sit in a quiet space and let your imagination work for you, as you prepare to move to "The Comfortable Zone of Confidence".

The Comfortable Zone of Confidence

In "The Comfortable Zone of Confidence" you will realize your innate abilities to achieve great things and value your self-worth. You will not allow other to negatively define you, nor allow them to make you feel uncomfortable. Your positive self-esteem will boost your level of confidence, because you will recognize your unique qualities and abilities to be your authentic self. The perceived thoughts and expressions of others will not cause you to shy away from unfamiliar people and social involvement. You will maintain courage to continue to believe in yourself and your abilities to live your life in peace and harmony. You will remind yourself that your personal character is as good as or even better than some of the people who you may encounter. Your confidence will become stronger as you face any fears and just behave in ways that are natural and comfortable for you.

Personal Pledge

I shall continue to maintain confidence, value my self-worth,

appreciate my unique character

and recognize my innate abilities to achieve great things.

The Uncomfortable Zone of Boredom

Boredom is a feeling of discontent and emptiness caused by not being involved in something interesting or gratifying to do. It can be caused by not having a meaningful purpose or a lack of personal fulfillment. Being in this zone may cause anxiety, depression, loneliness, anger, insecurity, irritability, sadness, self-destructive behavior and other personal uncomfortable feelings. Finding something meaningful and/or finding someone or some outside source to inspire and motivate a person to become actively involved may be needed to break the feeling of boredom. It is necessary to identify a meaningful purpose and make a commitment to become actively involved in an effort to move to "The Comfortable Zone of Involvement".

Prepare to Move Forward

It is important to think of things, people, events, talents, activities and other ideas that will help bring needed "Involvement". Sit in a quiet space and let your imagination work for you, as you prepare to move to "The Comfortable Zone of Involvement".

The Comfortable Zone of Involvement

In "The Comfortable Zone of Involvement" you will participate in personally rewarding and meaningful activities. You have the choice of solitary involvement in your own creative endeavor or an environment involving others. Your vision regarding the level of involvement is your decision. If you are a self- motivated person and you can find peace in your own private space, this may be your comfort zone. However, if you are more inclined to need the motivation of others, you may benefit from social interaction. In either case, this zone must offer personal growth and intellectual inspiration. Seek out a variety of activities that will keep you meaningfully involved and motivated. The field is wide open. However, it will take action on your part and making a selection from ideas that will inspire you to continue your involvement. You may try several things before settling into one thing. Just get out and put forth the effort. Do not return to "The Uncomfortable Zone of Boredom".

Personal Pledge

I shall replace boredom by being involved in an activity,

a series of activities or a creative project

that is personally rewarding and meaningfully inspiring.

The Uncomfortable Zone of Inferiority

Inferiority is a feeling of insecurity and feeling inadequate. It may involve the perception that one has of their own physical and/or mental shortcomings. The feeling of being weak, having certain limitations or being looked upon by others as 'not being adequate', are among some reasons that a person feels inferior. A person may become an "underachiever" and not even attempt to accomplish some of the things that they are capable of doing. On the other hand some may become overachievers because they are trying to prove that they can achieve 'above average tasks' and in the process they exceed their mental and/or physical limits and they experience "Burnout". It is important for anyone who perceives themselves as being inferior, to take action to move to "The Comfortable Zone of Competence".

Prepare to Move Forward

It is important to think of things, people, events, talents, activities and other ideas that will help bring needed "Competency". Sit in a quiet space and let your imagination work for you, as you prepare to move to "The Comfortable Zone of Competence".

The Comfortable Zone of Competence

In "The Comfortable Zone of Competence" you will recognize your own unique self-worth and practice self-respect. You will exercise your ability to perform within your own level of competency and skill levels. You will appreciate yourself as the individual that you are and not make yourself uncomfortable by attempting tasks that are too difficult. If you wish to, you may safely work to achieve new things that you aspire to achieve. You will explain your actions only when necessary. You will avoid anyone who does not have your best interest in mind. Over time your competency level will grow and you will show others that you deserve respect for your special personality. You will not place unrealistic expectations on yourself just to appease or pacify others. You will not allow anyone to intimidate you by making negative comments. Remember, no one is picture-perfect. Do not harm yourself just to prove otherwise.

Personal Pledge

I shall always appreciate myself for my own individual character
and be at peace within my own personal level of competence.

The Uncomfortable Zone of Frustration

Frustration is an emotional response when a person is annoyed, angry, disappointed and/or feeling any degree of irritation. As frustrations are elevated this emotion may lead to unhealthy behavior. There are times when attempting to place the blame on another should be re-examined, because it may be necessary to reform expectations. When wanting more out of life than someone is receiving, this can be another cause of frustration. So, options must be considered and resolved within the scope of reality. Staying in "The Uncomfortable Zone of Frustration" can be self-defeating and dangerous to your physical, mental, emotional and/or spiritual well-being. A resolution may require input from the people who you trust.

Prepare to Move Forward

It is important to think of things, people, events, talents, activities and other ideas that will help bring needed "Contentment". Sit in a quiet space and let your imagination work for you, as you prepare to move to "The Comfortable Zone of Contentment".

The Comfortable Zone of Contentment

In "The Comfortable Zone of Contentment" you will be welcomed by parents, family members, teachers, trusted friends, counselors and other community resources who have your best interest in mind. You will confide in the person who you feel will offer you the greatest comfort and understanding. They will help you to replace your negative thoughts with positive ones. They may even help you to find some "humor" in anything that might be causing your frustrations. They will help you to move beyond the current uncomfortable zone by creating a plan to resolve any issues and offer techniques that you can use to replace many negative feelings in the future. The plan includes calming activities such as: deep breathing exercises, nature walks, listening to your favorite music, reading a favorite book, journaling and any other appropriate activity that will keep you in "The Comfortable Zone of Contentment".

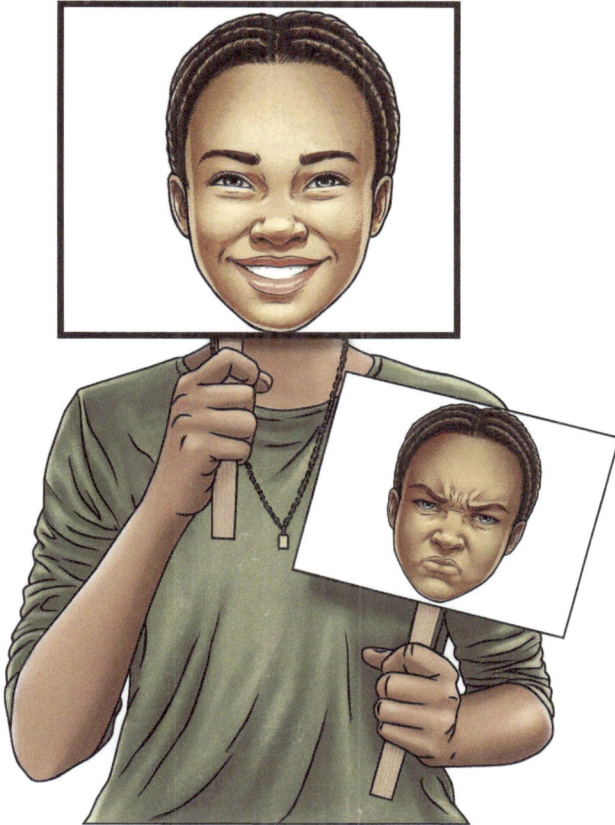

Personal Pledge

I shall continue to focus on realistic expectations of myself and others
and continue to maintain a vision of peace and contentment in my daily life

The Uncomfortable Zone of Mistrust

Mistrust may be a series of feelings that includes lack of confidence in something and/or someone, doubtfulness, suspicion, uncertainty, feelings of betrayal, etc. It may be a hunch or gut feeling that something or someone is not who you wish to be involved. These thoughts may be very beneficial when making decisions about relationships and other personal matters. Staying in this zone may provide the time to consider your feelings, gather the facts and strengthen your ability to move forward. This zone of mistrust can be uncomfortable but it may prove to be valuable. The key to opening the lock to escape this zone is in your hands. Value your instincts, your wise observations and prepare to move to "The Comfortable Zone of Trust".

Prepare to Move Forward

It is important to think of things, people, events, talents, activities and other ideas that will help bring needed feelings of "Trust". Sit in a quiet space and let your imagination work for you, as you prepare to move to "The Comfortable Zone of Trust".

The Comfortable Zone of Trust

In "The Comfortable Zone of Trust" you will feel an inner sense of peace and a greater awareness of the people, things and situations that offer you needed confidence and faith. You will experience a strong inner sense of who exhibits genuine appreciation, respect, acceptance and those who truly have your best interest in mind. You will know how to guard your secrets and innermost feelings until there is a complete conviction that there is no sign of mistrust. Your emotions will relax and you will feel relieved and become more involved when you experience feelings of sincere trust. You will decline any activities that do not align with your ethical values. . You will continue to evaluate your feelings and make wise choices that enable you to remain in your own personal "Comfortable Zone of Trust".

Personal Pledge

I shall avoid people and experiences that are not in my best interest.

I shall continue to recognize situations that make me feel unsafe or insecure

and continue to trust my instincts.

The Uncomfortable Zone of Repulsion

Repulsion is an emotional response to something and/or someone perceived to be offensive or unpleasant. There may be a feeling of disgust when responding to a person's behavior, their physical appearance, what and/or how they communicate, how they smell or even something that is unexplainable. Repulsion may be a reaction to any undesirable sight, taste, smell, touch, sound and/or unexpected event that is perceived to be a "turn off". This emotional response may cause a "Fight or flight" reaction. This emotion can be a valuable tool of protection and a sign to avoid or distance yourself from whatever the cause may be. It is important to quickly move to "The Comfortable Zone of Attraction".

Prepare to Move Forward

It is important to think of things, people, events, talents, activities and other ideas that will help bring needed feelings of "Attraction". Sit in a quiet space and let your imagination work for you, as you prepare to move to "The Comfortable Zone of Attraction".

The Comfortable Zone of Attraction

In "The Comfortable Zone of Attraction" you will sense a closeness and a desire to interact with someone and/or others on a more intellectual, emotional and/or appropriate physical level. When you encounter something that appeals to your sense of sight, taste, smell, touch, sound and/or some event, you will feel the chosen attraction that will bring desired peace and contentment. Look around and open yourself up to new experiences that are within your personal comfort zone. Continue to evaluate the situations, people and things that are in the safety zone of attraction. However, be aware of those who may attempt to cause emotional and/or physical harm to you. Always guard your reputation and do not compromise your personal integrity for any reason. Remember, just because something or someone "looks good" it still may not be a wise choice. Do not let your guard down.

Personal Pledge

My daily goal shall be to distance myself from
those people, things and situations that I am not attracted to
and remain in the zone that offers peace and contentment.

The Uncomfortable Zone of Fear

Fear is an emotional response to something that feels frightful about a person, a situation or anything that may cause potential harm or displeasure. Other words that can be associated with fear are nervous, scared, frightened, uneasy, panicky, apprehensive, horror, anxious, worried, concerned, etc. Some fears may offer a 'mental safety net' and may help someone to avoid something that might be a threat to a person's physical, mental, emotional and/or financial well-being. However, unjustified fears can hinder a person from doing something that may be personally beneficial. It is important to consider the nature of the perceived fear by moving into "The Comfortable Zone of Discovery".

Prepare to Move Forward

It is important to think of things, people, events, talents, activities and other ideas that will help to diminish the feelings of "Fear" and move into "The Comfortable Zone of Discovery". Sit in a quiet space and let your imagination work for you, as you prepare to move to "The Comfortable Zone of Discovery".

The Comfortable Zone of Discovery

In "The Comfortable Zone of Discovery" you will freely explore the underlining reasons that may be causing you to be fearful. You will take time to determine why you are hesitant or unwilling to face who or what the real cause might be. You will encounter people who will help you to validate your feelings and they will introduce some meaningful ways for you to reverse your fears. You may decide to join a "Support Group" that will offer understanding and mental preparation for moving forward. You will relax and trust your ability to move at a pace that is comfortable for you. Reversing fears takes time and the need to understand if this emotion is in your best interest. Determine if it really is a feeling that you should work to resolve. Let "The Zone of Discovery" provide you the opportunity to clarify your feelings.

Personal Pledge

I shall take time to explore the reasons that I experience the emotions of fear
and determine if the reasons are valid and for my protection.

I will explore ways to reverse any unjustified fears.

The Uncomfortable Zone of Despair

Despair is a feeling that someone has when they have lost any degree of hope. Other relatable feelings are depression, gloom, misery, anguish, desperation, anxiety, dejection, worry, etc. This feeling may be brought on by current events or about thinking about past events. When a person has lost hope and cannot see a peaceful way forward, this feeling immobilizes the person and they make no attempts to regain optimism. This zone of despair is a very perilous place to be. Personal habits (hygiene) and other unhealthy behavior may cause additional grief. It is critical to seek help and move to "The Comfortable Zone of Hope".

Prepare to Move Forward

It is important to think of things, people, events, talents, activities and other ideas that will help to diminish the feelings of "Despair" and move into "The Comfortable Zone of Hope". Sit in a quiet space and let your imagination work for you, as you prepare to move to "The Comfortable Zone of Hope".

The Comfortable Zone of Hope

In "The Comfortable Zone of Hope" you will experience an atmosphere of positivity and achieve the mental insight to accomplish your goals and ambitions. Your newfound confidence and faith in yourself will sustain you. Retreat to your personal space and engage in personal reflections to gain a positive outlook. Seek help from the people who will provide any needed support. Take time to identify your purpose and the things that will keep you in the zone of hope and contentment. Write these things down and establish realistic priorities. Do not over-burden yourself with too many things at a time. Continue to believe in yourself and practice the behavior that benefits you in your quest for hope. Do not be so hard on yourself and do not allow others to push you beyond your own personal desires and limitations.

Personal Pledge

I shall continue to focus my attention on maintaining hope and optimism and accept needed help from others who have my best interest in mind.

The Uncomfortable Zone of Sleeplessness

Sleeplessness is also known as insomnia. It is a condition where a person has difficulty falling asleep and/or staying asleep when it is their designated bedtime. Sleeplessness may cause irritability, low concentration, low energy, mood swings, restlessness, and other undesirable behavior. Not being able to calm the mind because of too many unresolved issues and personal struggles can certainly be the root cause of sleeplessness. One very important consideration may be a medical issue that must be attended to by a professional. Consider the sleeping environment. Is it too hot or too cold? Is there too much noise? Is there too much light? Is there fear of the dark? Other factors include caffeine or alcohol intake, side-effects of drugs or medicines, troubled relationships, body pain, electronic devices, cell phones, over-all stress and dissatisfaction with life in general. This is not a unique problem but it is serious if it is long-standing. Sleep deprivation can lead to serious mental, physical, emotional and financial disruptions in one's life. It is important to quickly move to "The Comfortable Zone of Restfulness".

Prepare to Move Forward

It is important to think of things, people, events, talents, activities and other ideas that will help to diminish the behavior of "Sleeplessness" and move into "The Comfortable Zone Restfulness". Sit in a quiet space and let your imagination work, as you prepare to move to "The Comfortable Zone of Restfulness".

The Comfortable Zone of Restfulness

In "The Comfortable Zone of Restfulness" you will sit and identify the issues that are causing you to experience sleeplessness. You will determine your ability to personally resolve the problem. Reflect on how and who may be required for any needed assistance. You will begin to make any changes that you can personally alter. (Review those changes as mentioned above) If noise is a factor, would earplugs help? Try deep breathing exercises and focus on calming the mind prior to bedtime. Eliminate unpleasant thoughts. Avoid eating or drinking at least 2 hours before bedtime. Wear comfortable sleeping attire. Take time to remove unnecessary items and other distractions from your bed. An organized environment and one that is free from clutter offers a more restful atmosphere. Seek any professional services and not allow "Sleep Deprivation" to linger.   To remain in "The Comfortable Zone of Restfulness" you must continue to work with all of your support resources. This list includes your parents, family, teachers, school counselors, neighbors, friends, medical staff, school nurses and others who may assist in the resolutions to your sleeplessness.

Personal Pledge

I shall continue to maintain the behavior that will help

to keep me in "The Zone of Restfulness"

and seek the needed help from my list of people who will provide support.

The Uncomfortable Zone of Agitation

Agitation is a state of extreme distress brought on by some physical, mental, emotional, and/or spiritual irritation. It can range from mild to severe. It may very well be caused by a medical condition, some stressful encounter or some unexplained reason. There are a wide range of indicators that a person who is agitated may exhibit. They may be experiencing inner tensions that are not visible to an untrained observer. Some visible indicators include vocal expressions of anger, unusual facial expressions, restlessness, fidgeting, body rocking, physical pacing, throwing things in anger, abusive behavior, a rapid heartbeat, cold sweats, hostility, confusion and any other unusual human behaviors. Any display of agitation must be recognized as serious and should be dealt with immediately. Many people who are severely agitated become a threat to themselves and society. Everyone must be aware of the need to immediately move from "The Zone of Agitation" and move to "The Comfortable Zone of Peacefulness" for their own safety and the safety of others.

Prepare to Move Forward

It is important to think of things, people, events, talents, activities and other ideas that will help to diminish the feelings of "Agitation" and move into "The Comfortable Zone Peacefulness". Sit in a quiet space and let your imagination work, as you prepare to move to "The Comfortable Zone of Peacefulness".

The Comfortable Zone of Peacefulness

In "The Comfortable Zone of Peacefulness" you will now experience feeling of relaxation and you are now in control of your behavior. This is your time to explore the issues, situation, people and the environments that may have caused you to become agitated. Consider the ways that you will reach a peaceful resolution. You will dismiss any feelings of displeasure and alienation. The people are here to help you to make wise decisions that allow you to peacefully move forward. A trusted person who is trained in "Conflict Resolutions" is here to help you. There will be no need to continue to hold any negative feelings of agitation. These feelings will only destroy the potential for a peaceful life. All of your actions going forward will be supported by the people who understand your feelings and are here to support you. They include your parents, your family, your teachers, school counselors, friends, etc. Now, take a series of deep breaths and let your mind create images of being in a place of personal peace and tranquility. Let nothing draw you away from "The Comfortable Zone of Peacefulness".

Personal Pledge

I shall practice being in control of my behavior and my emotions.

I shall focus on the comfortable feelings of inner calm and peacefulness.

The Uncomfortable Zone of Ungratefulness

Ungratefulness is a behavior that is reflected in a failure to express gratitude and/or appreciation for the things received and/or to the people who extend help in providing anything that may help to make life better for another. A sense of entitlement and/or selfishness may cause ungrateful behavior. Some people tend to be "takers" and not "givers". Unwillingness to compromise and wanting things to go their way, a disregard for the sacrifices that others have made is a sign of immaturity and ungratefulness. An ungrateful person may soon learn that this behavior will not win friends. Taking others for granted and thinking that this behavior is acceptable is a mistake. They will soon experience feelings of isolation and loneliness. They will benefit by moving to "The Comfortable Zone of Gratefulness"

Prepare to Move Forward

It is important to think of things, people, events, talents, activities and other ideas that will help to diminish the feelings and behavior of "Ungratefulness" and move into "The Comfortable Zone Gratefulness". Sit in a quiet space and let your imagination work as you reflect on your ungrateful behavior and prepare to move to "The Comfortable Zone of Gratefulness".

The Comfortable Zone of Gratefulness

In "The Comfortable Zone of Gratefulness" I will begin to feel a deep sense of appreciation as I think about all of the people and things that I have in my life. I now take notice of what I have because of the help and sacrifices that have been made to provide for me. I am remembering the many words of encouragement, the people who have made me aware of my selfish behavior, the friends that are no longer around and the unkind things that I have said. In this zone I now am taking time to reflect on how my disregard for others is the reason that I have been feeling unfulfilled and acting so ungrateful. I am going to extend words of appreciation to include: thank you, I appreciate what you have done for me, this means a lot and other words to express my gratitude and my gratefulness. I shall also make personal phone calls, handwritten notes, special cards and extend other thoughtful gestures. "The Comfortable Zone of Gratefulness" is where I will practice showing my gratitude.

Personal Pledge

I shall continue to express my appreciation to the people
who provide things, support, encouragement (both big and small)
and for all of their efforts that help to sustain and improve my life.

The Uncomfortable Zone of Overwhelmed

Overwhelmed refers to having feelings, thoughts and/or having a sensation that something is difficult to manage. Having too many unresolved issues and not enough resources to handle what needs to be done and feelings of "being at your wit's end" can be very stressful, physically and emotionally draining. In this very tense zone a person may have difficulty concentrating, may develop body aches, headaches, low energy, loss of interest in their favorite things and immerse themselves in unhealthy behavior. It is critical to move to "The Comfortable Zone of Organization".

Prepare to Move Forward

It is important to think of things, people, events, talents, activities and other ideas that will help to diminish the feelings of being "Overwhelmed" and move into "The Comfortable Zone of Organization". Sit in a quiet space and let your imagination work as you reflect on your feelings of being "Overwhelmed" and prepare to move to "The Comfortable Zone of Organization".

The Comfortable Zone of Organization

In "The Comfortable Zone of Organization" you are now feeling a sense of relief and the burdens of being overwhelmed are now being reduced. The people are here to offer you much needed support, you are in a state of mind to develop a plan to reduce your personal workload, you will discuss certain responsibilities and feel the stress rolling away. You will make a realistic list of your priorities and not over-schedule or over-promise when time is limited. Your school and your studies must be at the top of your list. You will now organize your environment and remove all clutter and distractions. You must wisely use your time and your abilities to complete tasks in a timely manner. This means avoiding procrastination and not waiting until the last minute to tackle any necessary responsibilities.

Personal Pledge

I shall continue to maintain organization

and set real priorities in my daily life.

I shall continue to wisely use my time to avoid feeling overwhelmed.

The Uncomfortable Zone of Uncertainty

Uncertainty refers to feelings of being undecided, unsettled and lacking confidence in oneself and/or any decisions that have to be made. It also includes having doubts, being suspicious or mistrustful about a person or situation. Any form of skepticism may render a person to be uncertain. Uncertainty may cause a person to respond slowly about deciding on important issues and this will delay progress. It is necessary to clarify any facts in order to trust the accuracy and quickly move to "The Comfortable Zone of Confidence".

Prepare to Move Forward

It is important to think of things, people, events, talents, activities and other ideas that will help to diminish the feelings of "Uncertainty" and move into "The Comfortable Zone of Confidence". Sit in a quiet space and let your imagination work as you reflect on your feelings of "Uncertainty" and prepare to move to "The Comfortable Zone of Confidence".

The Comfortable Zone of Confidence

In "The Comfortable Zone of Confidence" you will now take time to gather all of the information that you need in order to restore your faith, trust and belief in yourself. This will allow you to make wise decisions and remove self-doubt. In this zone the people and other resources are here to offer you needed support. They are offering reassurance and are here to guide you along the pathways of positivity and reveal the ways that you will be strengthened by your various encounters with life and not suffer defeat. You will set realistic goals and expectations. You will take one step at a time and feel your confidence continue to strengthen. Temporary setbacks will not overthrow you. "The Comfortable Zone of Confidence" is your special space and you will continue to stake your claim.

Personal Pledge

I shall remember that confidence is built over a span of time.

It may include "Trial and Error".

So, any setbacks will not overthrow or defeat me.

The Uncomfortable Zone of Being Terrified

Terrified is a response to being frightened, scared and thrown into a panic. There are different levels of dread and fear in terrifying situations. When seeing something or someone who appears too unfamiliar, a distorted image, a dream, an unexplained illusion, something that appears unexpectedly or experiencing a flashback, are events that can certainly cause someone to become terrified. An intentional or unintentional reaction may cause someone to harm themselves and/or someone else. If a person continues to have flashbacks from some previous encounters, they must seek professional help. This can be a 'traumatic disorder' and must be taken seriously. Any delays will deplete a person, physically, emotionally, mentally, spiritually and/or financially. Any extreme fears or phobias can immobilize a person and affect the quality of their lives. It is important to quickly move to "The Comfortable Zone of Calmness" and begin the healing process.

Prepare to Move Forward

It is important to think of things, people, events, talents, activities and other ideas that will help to diminish the feelings of being "Terrified" and move into "The Comfortable Zone of Calmness". Sit in a quiet space and let your imagination work as you reflect on your feelings of being "Terrified" and prepare to move to "The Comfortable Zone of Calmness".

The Comfortable Zone of Calmness

In "The Comfortable Zone of Calmness" you are now surrounded by the people who will help you to understand the reality of your feelings of being terrified. This environment of peace and calm will help you to tone down the intensity and allow you to experience mental and emotional healings. You will be given the tools needed to protect yourself by qualified professionals. You will confide in your parents and/or guardians, medical doctors, teachers, school leaders, counselors, mental health specialists and other community resources. You will be taught effective ways to confront any terrifying person and situation. "The Comfortable Zone of Calmness" is you space to experience serenity and clear your mind of any unnecessary trauma.

Personal Pledge

I shall practice remaining calm in the presence of terrifying situations.

A calm mind allows me to be in control of my emotions and my actions,

in order to make wise decisions about protecting myself.

The Uncomfortable Zone of Guilt

Guilt is a response to a person feeling that they have done something wrong or unwise and they worry about how to express their remorse. This unresolved situation is weighing on the person and they are uncertain about how to approach the issue. Depending upon the magnitude of the guilt, their concern about the outcome can affect a person physically, mentally, emotionally and/or spiritually. The more people who are involved and the scope of the offense, the more intense the feelings of guilt might become. There are a number of offenses that a person might commit that might cause feelings of guilt. Some include, taking advantage of an innocent person, taking or stealing, mistreating others and any form of deception or wrongdoing. Something as simple as not calling a friend when they are expecting a call can make a person have feelings of guilt. Some people are more sensitive to being responsible than others. So, a more caring and responsible person may have feelings of guilt more than someone who is inclined to be selfish and uncaring. For the healing of guilt, it is important to move to "The Comfortable Zone of Ownership" and make amends.

Prepare to Move Forward

It is important to think of things, people, events, talents, activities and other ideas that will help to diminish the feelings of "Guilt" and move into "The Comfortable Zone of Ownership". Sit in a quiet space and let your imagination work as you reflect on your feelings of "Guilt" and prepare to move to "The Comfortable Zone of Ownership".

The Comfortable Zone of Ownership

In "The Comfortable Zone of Ownership" you will finally confess your feeling of remorse and seek any needed forgiveness. You will now offer to make amends and participate in repairing anything or any relationship that can be repaired. This zone may prove to be intense but it is necessary as you attempt to clear your conscience and lift the burden of guilt. Once you have done all that you can think of, it might take time for the situation to clear but you must be willing to accept the final outcome with grace and humility. In this zone you will learn powerful lessons of sensitivity to the needs of others and making timely confessions as you avoid the heavy burden of guiltiness.

Personal Pledge

I shall remember how to minimize the burden of guilt
and practice taking ownership of my faults, sooner rather than later.

The Uncomfortable Zone of Bewilderment

Bewilderment is caused by being confused, puzzled or unable to understand a situation or a person. In this emotional state things just don't make sense. A person can become upset and agitated. Being so preoccupied and unable to clearly figure things out makes it difficult to wisely make decisions. Some things can be very difficult to understand, can cause someone to waste valuable time and energy and can become what some call "a brain drain". Having a fixation on issues that are out of a person's control and field of understanding is mentally exhausting. Avoid wasting time and energy in "The Uncomfortable Zone of Bewilderment" and swiftly move to "The Comfortable Zone of Contentment".

Prepare to Move Forward

It is important to think of things, people, events, talents, activities and other ideas that will help to diminish the feelings of "Bewilderment" and move into "The Comfortable Zone of Contentment". Sit in a quiet space and let your imagination work as you reflect on your uncomfortable feelings of "Bewilderment" and prepare to move to "The Comfortable Zone of Contentment".

The Comfortable Zone of Contentment

In "The Comfortable Zone of Contentment" you will not spend any more time or energy second guessing or dwelling on any nonsense that is beyond your control or comprehension. In this zone you will take a deep breath and exhale, as you change your attitude to acceptance and contentment. Let go and focus on understanding that you cannot comprehend nor control everything in life. Bewilderment is a distraction from focusing on the more pleasurable things that are in store for you personally. Become aware of the need to remain in "The Comfortable Zone of Contentment" for peace of mind and your personal refuge.

Personal Pledge

I shall only focus on the issues and things that are within my ability to control
and embrace those people and things that offer me personal contentment

The Uncomfortable Zone of Nervousness

Nervousness is caused by a reaction to some unpleasant situation, issue or encounter. There may be concern over some unresolved problems and this triggers anxiety, agitation, restlessness, stress, uneasiness and an overall tense response. In this state it may cause a person to experience a rapid heartbeat, shallow breathing, body tremors, hand tremors, disorientation and other unusual behavior. A person who is experiencing nervousness should be helped to calm down and resolve the underlining reason for this emotional reaction. This is a symptom that something must be done to quickly move to "The Comfortable Zone of Relaxation".

Prepare to Move Forward

It is important to think of things, people, events, talents, activities and other ideas that will help to diminish the feelings of "Nervousness" and move into "The Comfortable Zone of Relaxation". Sit in a quiet space and let your imagination work as you reflect on your uncomfortable feelings of "Nervousness" and prepare to move to "The Comfortable Zone of Relaxation".

The Comfortable Zone of Relaxation

In "The Comfortable Zone of Relaxation" you will sit or recline in a comfortable space. Close your eyes and begin to take nice slow deep breaths, in through your nose, hold for 5 seconds and slowly exhale through the lips. You will now imagine a tranquil place where you can feel calm and total relaxation. Hold this image until you feel peace and emotional harmony. Engage in positive "Self-talk" and reassure yourself that the experience of any anxiety can be resolved with positive thinking and positive actions. Take time to compose yourself and think of any resources that may be needed to resolve the situation, as you continue to remain in the "The Comfortable Zone of Relaxation". Say, "If IT IS TO BE IT IS UP TO ME". You must claim this zone and make it your personal refuge.

Personal Pledge

I shall continue to focus on relaxation and calmness
and practice a series of deep breathing exercises
to help keep me in "The Zone of Relaxation"
when encountering any unpleasant situations.

The Uncomfortable Zone of Selfishness

Selfishness is a behavior where someone is excessively concerned about themselves and their needs. They show little esteem for the feelings and needs of others. They tend to express limited or no appreciation for the things that are done for them. Some people are predisposed to being selfish and some learn this behavior from the actions of others. Selfishness can be very destructive to maintaining good relationships. By acting in "self-centered ways" it may appear to be a sign of feeling superior. However, it may reveal a person's feelings of inferiority. In any case, this behavior and attitude can alienate those who are turned off by this exhibition of selfishness. A selfish person could certainly benefit more by moving to "The Comfortable Zone of Thoughtfulness".

Prepare to Move Forward

It is important to think of things, people, events, talents, activities and other ideas that will help to diminish the feelings and actions of "Selfishness" and move into "The Comfortable Zone of Thoughtfulness". Sit in a quiet space and let your imagination work as you reflect on your uncomfortable feelings and actions of "Selfishness" and prepare to move to "The Comfortable Zone of Thoughtfulness"

The Comfortable Zone of Thoughtfulness

In "The Comfortable Zone of Thoughtfulness" you will recognize the value in being concerned about the feelings, needs and well-being of others. You will practice expressing appreciation, showing respect, extending service to those in need, showing politeness and extending kind gestures that reflect genuine thoughtfulness. You will take time to listen to others, write personal notes of appreciation and gratitude, make phone calls to check on family, friends and others who merit your attention and discontinue any conduct that may reflect any selfish behavior. You will continue to reside in "The Comfortable Zone of Thoughtfulness". You will feel rewarded with a deep sense of personal pride as you extend acts of kindness and thoughtfulness toward others.

Personal Pledge

I shall continue to respect the needs, feelings
and the well-being of the people in my life.
I shall always express appreciation and thoughtfulness
in my day-to-day interactions with others.

The Uncomfortable Zone of Speechlessness

Speechlessness is being unable to quickly express feelings in appropriate words and in a timely manner. A person may become completely unable to say anything if experiencing some trauma, a head injury or injury to their vocal cords. This requires immediate medical attention or a call to 911. Less severe causes of speechless may be a sudden surprise, intense anger or temporary disorientation. A person who stutters will become speechless as they attempt to collect their thoughts. There are other medical conditions that may also render a person speechless. This experience can be very uncomfortable because they may have encounters with people who tease them. Insensitivity of others is on the rise and increases the number of people who make life uncomfortable for others. Effective communication is important to a person's well-being. It is essential to determine the reasons and/or the severity for speechlessness and move to "The Comfortable Zone of Articulation".

Prepare to Move Forward

It is important to think of things, people, events, talents, activities and other ideas that will help to diminish the feelings and causes of "Speechlessness" and move into "The Comfortable Zone of Articulation". Sit in a quiet space and let your imagination work as you reflect on your uncomfortable feelings and the causes of "Speechlessness" and prepare to move to "The Comfortable Zone of Articulation".

The Comfortable Zone of Articulation

In "The Comfortable Zone of Articulation" you and/or a qualified person will determine the severity of your inability to be coherent in responding in a timely manner. You will seek or have someone seek medical help if there is some trauma or head injury. If it is determined that there is no need for any intervention you may enjoy being in this zone as you relax and have a good laugh. It is wise to post emergency numbers and inform others and remind them of any needed actions just in case. Always remember to call 911 if there is a real emergency. It is important to stay calm and do not panic. A calm mind is important to being able to articulate the circumstances when help might be needed.

Personal Pledge

I shall not be alarmed if becoming speechless

and will remain calm and not have feelings of panic or anxiety.

The Uncomfortable Zone of Exhaustion

Exhaustion causes a person to feel physically, mentally and/or emotionally drained and lack the energy and motivation to accomplish tasks. This may be caused by too much physical exertion, not having enough support, being stressed, being sleep deprived, nutritional imbalances, boredom, environmental contamination, a medical condition and other issues that have not been diagnosed. Being in a state of exhaustion can compromise the quality of a person's life. Their life can spiral out of control and create a backlog of unattended responsibilities. When people over-extend themselves and not enough time to fulfill their obligations, this leads to exhaustion. Overpromising and not being able to deliver causes stress and anxiety. It is important to move to "The Comfortable Zone of Being Energized".

Prepare to Move Forward

It is important to think of things, people, events, talents, activities and other ideas that will help to diminish the feelings and actions of "Exhaustion" and move into "The Comfortable Zone of Being Energized". Sit in a quiet space and let your imagination work as you reflect on your uncomfortable feelings and actions of "Exhaustion" and prepare to move to "The Comfortable Zone of Being Energized".

The Comfortable Zone of Being Energized

In "The Comfortable Zone of Being Energized" you will seek help in ruling out any medical conditions and do what is needed to safely and medically restore your energy. You will discuss any issues that you know to be the cause of your exhaustion. Have these discussions with your parents, teachers, counselors, school nurses, family members, coaches and any others who are a part of your inner circle. You will not take anything or do anything that is not prescribed by your medical doctor. You will modify your behavior by getting 6 – 8 hours of sleep each night, cut down on "Junk Foods", exercise daily and have a meaningful sense of purpose.

See page 62 "Twenty-Five Energy Robbers"

Personal Pledge

I shall get 6-8 hours of sleep each night,

eat less "Junk Food", exercise daily,

organize my life and not participate in any unhealthy behavior.

The Uncomfortable Zone of Being Defeated

Defeated is a feeling that a person might have when they think that they have failed at something or they have experienced a personal loss. If things are not going right or not going as they expect them to, they experience this feeling of being defeated. Some may even sink into a state of sadness or even serious depression. People can feel defeated if they experience losing in a game, in a contest, in financial matters, in a relationship, not achieving academically, losing personal possessions and the list is endless. Any issue that a person cannot personally solve and/or achieve can cause a person to feel defeated. Some people are more competitive than others and they are more prone to suffer defeat and respond as "a poor looser", with displays of anger, rage and other displays of disappointment. It is critical to move into "The Comfortable Zone of Feeling Undefeated".

Prepare to Move Forward

It is important to think of things, people, events, talents, activities and other ideas that will help to diminish the uncomfortable feelings and actions of feeling "Defeated" and move into "The Comfortable Zone of Feeling Undefeated". Sit in a quiet space and let your imagination work as you reflect on your uncomfortable feelings and actions of being "Defeated" and prepare to move to "The Comfortable Zone of Feeling Undefeated".

The Comfortable Zone of Feeling Undefeated

In "The Comfortable Zone of Feeling Undefeated" you will reflect on the high expectations that you may have had and focus on any actions that were exhibited to the best of your abilities. You will not beat up on yourself. Rather, you will use your energy to learn what needs to be done as you move forward. You will no longer be emotionally consumed with any feelings of defeat but you will plan for future adventures and tasks that you can approach with a positive attitude and optimism. You will practice good sportsmanship and not be consumed by feelings of "defeat" or juvenile displays of anger, rage or other unbecoming behavior. Use all of your positive energy to improve your skills in the areas that require your attention and feel a calm sense of personal achievements when you know that you have done your best.

Personal Pledge

I shall continue to spend my time and energy

practicing ways to improve skills in all aspects of my life,

that involve my participation.

(School work, home chores, sports, relationships, extracurricular activities, etc.)

Ten Things to Consider for Personal and Interpersonal Success

1. Love: First love, respect and care for yourself. Love the body that you are in. Love the mind that you shall continue to cultivate. Maintain love for others who are there for you.

2. Flexibility: Most things are not 'set in stone'. Minds can change, situations can change and people can change. Be aware of the need for you to change based on circumstances. Have an exit plan, just in case.

3. Compromise: It may not always be about doing things your way. Be willing to agree to "a middle ground" in certain situations.

4. Observe: Continue to see and take mental notes of things, situations and events that you encounter. Pay attention to when it is necessary to get out of harm's way.

5. Listen: Continue to open your ears and regard the wisdom of those who have lived and had many life experiences. Listen and learn.

6. Management: Continue to make the best use of precious time and other available resources.

7. Think: Always put "Your Thinking Cap On" before taking any drastic actions. Continue to think about things that might affect your life if you make any unwise moves. That includes the present and the future.

8. Perseverance: If you are determined to accomplish something good, continue to work diligently to achieves your goals. Determination and diligence are important to completing the tasks.

9. Respect: Continue to practice respect and appreciation for your body, mind, emotions and spirit. Do not take anything, drink anything or do anything that will cause you harm. Show appreciation for others in order to maintain their respect for you.

10. Networking: Last but not least continue to associate with others who work to achieve worthwhile goals. Seek out those who may have similar goals and be a source of encouragement to them.

Twenty-Five Energy Robbers

The following situations, conditions and circumstances have the potential to rob you of the energy that you need in order to accomplish day-to-day tasks. Can you identify any that may be robbing you? Work on those that are and take back your power.

. Sleep Deprivation
. Sensory Over-Load
. Dehydration
. Over-Scheduling
. Decision Fatigue
. Financial Deprivation
. Mental Fatigue
. Physical Fatigue
. Emotional Fatigue
. Nutritional Imbalances
. Lack of Exercise and Movements
. Lack of Social Interaction
. Lack of Fun, Laughter and Joy
. Mundane and Board Lifestyle
. Non-Participation in Special Interest
. Uninviting Environment and Surroundings
. Lack of Cultural Involvement
. Declining Health (Poor Elimination)
. Poor Hygiene
. Feelings of Being Unfulfilled
. Poor Self-Esteem
. Mistreatment by Others
. Lack of Needed Resources and Information
. Innate Fears
. Lack of Love for Self and/or Others

Triggers for Anger, Rage and/or Antagonism

The following are some of the circumstances that may cause people to have negative feelings and could very well cause them to lose control of their behavior. It is important to be aware of the issues and work to eliminate any negative feelings that may trigger anger, rage and/or antagonism.

1. Lack of education, information, and/or poor communication skills
2. Inferiority complex
3. Disappointing experiences (from childhood to the present)
4. Lack of good examples or good role models for dealing with anger, etc.
5. Being economically deprived
6. Feeling disconnected, ignored, and/or neglected
7. Feeling misunderstood
8. Rough treatment and/or feeling manipulated
9. Unfairly judged and/or being wrongly blamed
10. Lack of a Spiritual Connection
11. Having no meaningful purpose
12. Feeling trapped, threatened or helpless
13. Being harassed, teased or bullied
14. Harmonal changes
15. Lack of basic resources
16. Innate fears (fear of failure or success)
17. Lack of effective problem-solving skills
18. Identity crisis (gender confusion)
19. Lack of hope or lack of trust
20. Dysfunctional family
21. Dysfunctional community
22. Undesirable isolation
23. Feeling emotionally broken
24..A failed support system
25. Drugs, alcohol and/or other substance abuse
26. Wanting more out of life
27. A medical condition
28. Feeling defeated, worthless and/or beyond redemption
29..Lack of compassion, empathy or humility for others
30..Experiencing bigotry and racial bias
31..Feeling unloved and/or unlovable
32..Inflated ego, vane, and self-centered personality
33..Lack of internal peace, self-love and/or self-respect
34..Lack of self-control
35..Lack of basic survival skill

Word Power

Words are powerful. They influence our beliefs, our actions, our mental programing, our quest to achieve and our desires to live a life that is filled with harmony and joy. We truly respond to what we think and believe. Single words can be powerful when that stand alone or when they are grouped into a sentence.

The following list of words are in random order and are intended to elicit positive thought and lead to positive actions. Take time to scan the list and focus on the descriptive words that resonate with your special desires to achieve. At first, less may be best. In given time you will achieve more and more. This is intended to be "a work in progress".

• Educated	Survivor	Faithful	Courageous
• Hopeful	Believer	Peaceful	Charitable
• Strong	Appreciative	Contented	Honest
• Joyous	Resilient	Grateful	Thrilled
• Upbeat	Blessed	Cheerful	Fortunate
• Satisfied	Graceful	Merry	Dynamic
• Energized	Cultured	Patient	Sharing
• Comforted	Blissful	Powerful	Gleeful
• Alert	Playful	Effervescent	Spirited
• Passionate	Unselfish	Enthusiastic	Friendly
• Vivacious	Prosperous	Organized	Lucky
• Resourceful	Auspicious	Lighthearted	Vibrant
• Buoyant	Calm	Secure	Healthy
• Rested	Delightful	Gracious	Radiant
• Restored	Invigorated	Mellow	Warmhearted
• Wholesome	Inspired	Balanced	Jubilant
• Worthy	Adequate	Competent	Prepared
• Qualified	Colorful	Desirable	Successful
• Thriving	Wealthy	Victorious	Experienced
• Jovial	Harmonious	Tranquil	Sunny
• Comical	Entertaining	Festive	Unruffled
• Exhilarated	Industrious	Provocative	Talented
• Encouraged	Stimulated	Favored	Optimistic
• Gifted	Prudent	Eager	Euphoric
• Enchanted	Powerful	Fearless	Determined
• Motivated	Creative	Loveable	Special
• Unique	Triumphant	Willing	Empathetic
• Truthful	Considerate	Survivor	Civil
• Curious	Inventive	Sentimental	Supportive
• Positive	Focused	Nurturing	Forgiving
• Unstoppable	Sociable	Outgoing	Humane

Feelings Do Matter

Feeling sometimes
may be hidden inside.
Some feelings
we should never attempt to hide.
Not even for the sake
of our personal pride.

It is so much better to avoid
keeping them bottled up.
When holding too long
they may soon erupt.
Then they will quickly overflow
your tiny little cup.

So, feelings must be
effectively attended to.
It is a must that you find
positive things to do.
In all things remember,
"To thine own self you must be true".

Feelings Do Matter to Me and to You

JOY to the Rescue

Welcome an infusion
of good old pure JOY
to energize your human soul.
This feeling of pure JOY
in the human heart
will never ever grow old.

To those who doubt the value of JOY,
they should try it on for fit and size.
They will soon discover
JOY will deliver a very pleasant surprise.

JOY living in the human heart
will leave no space or time
to grumble, moon or groan.
JOY serves up inspiration for you
to better love yourself and others too.
There will be no incentive
to cast a hateful stone.

JOY to the rescue.
Invite JOY into your heart.
Celebrate renewed feelings of harmony,
peace, happiness and bliss.
Make a list of all the JOYFUL things
and seal it with a kiss.

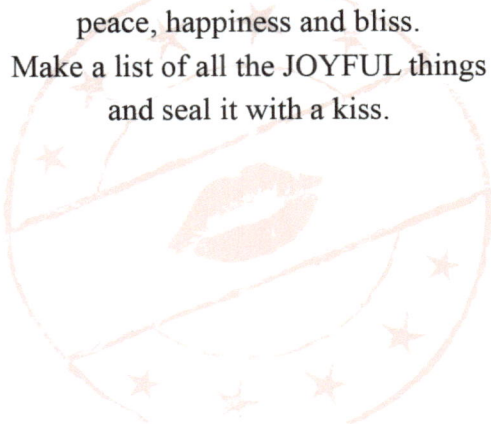

I Can't Run.....I Can't Hide

I can't run,
I can't hide
from the person that is living inside.

They follow me all of the time.
Where I go,
they always know.

They peek inside
my every thought.
They even know what I've been taught.

I must always
do things right
'cos I'm always in their sight

I must accept that they will
always be a part of me.
For this has become my reality.

~~~~~~~~~~~~~~~~

I Can't Run,
I Can't Hide
from the person living inside.

Keep Your Eyes on the Prize

Keep your eyes on the prize
and have a masterplan.
Trust that you can achieve it.
Oh yes you can.

Your mind may envision
the prize of your desires.
Now, are you willing to do the work
that your plan requires?

A prize is not always given
simply based upon a wish.
So, get ready to roll up your sleeves
and give your plan that needed push.

Get all of your resources
in a neat, organized row.
Wake up everyday
ready to go, go, go.

The prize may be something
that you truly recognize.
It may even appear
in an unfamiliar disguise.

The Universe sometimes awards
the prize with a timely delay.
So, patience and a longer timeline
may come into play.

Don't Hate Me – Please Help Me

This is a story about a 7th grade boy named Billy

School is just so hard for me.
I feel like a tree limb without a tree.
The lessons go by much too fast.
I know that the teacher would like to put me in a "Body Cast".
I fear that I will never fit.
I just can't get the hang of it.
When for myself I try to defend,
I get into trouble in the end.
So, when I drop out for a day,
They call it "Playing Hooky" anyway.
My mom has to work, dad ain't around.
No other family adult can be found.
I really want to find a place to fit.
Just can't come up with the needed wit.
I don't feel that I'll ever win.
Where can I get help with ways to fit in?
I know they want to throw me out.
I just want to scream and shout.
I wish that I could finally be heard.
In my defense – I have not been allowed to say a word.
Now, today a counselor will decide my fate.
As for now, I just have to sit in his office and wait.
My mom had to take off from work.
I know that she thinks that I am a "Jerk".
God, I hope that everyone will understand,
I'm still a young boy – who can't think like a man.

(Continued on the next page)

So confused am I, while being rejected.
Feeling misunderstood, hated and unprotected.
What if I can't get my life to turn out right?
I still have bad dreams most every night.
Now, the counselor calls for my mom and me to come in.
I feel like I'm walking into "The Lion's Den".
On his desk is a thick folder containing stuff about me.
He opens it up for my mom to see.
A frown comes across my mom's face.
Oh, I wish that I could run away from this place.
As I hold my head down looking at the floor,
I have deep thoughts about running out of the door.
My mind now goes to another place and time.
I expect them to team up on me as if I had committed a crime.
My attention returns to the room when hearing my name.
Every offense is mine and I have to take the blame.
I was asked, "Why do you do so many things to offend?"
"You must realize that you will be punished in the end".
"Why do you not give your assignment's your very best?"
"Why do you continue to fail every test?"
"Why do you think that things are funny when they are not?"
Oh boy, they both have me on the spot.
"Why do you think that fighting is a way to settle a score?"
I know that they could come up with so much more.
I am a boy who has made more than one mistake.
How much more of this can I take?
I know that they won't really like what I have to say.
Well, I have to say it anyway.

(Continued on the next page)

I have always felt that I don't belong.
Wish that I could put the words into a song.
I am not the only kid who feels so out of place.
It makes my actions appear to be a disgrace.
At home, I never get a warm smile.
I have come to conclude that it is my mom's regular style.
I can't remember the last time that I was given a nice hug.
Any contact is a morning tug.
It is hard to wake up to face another day.
Most kids look to jump out of bed to learn and play.
I really want to feel more love and less hate.
Please, please help me before it is too late.
I really do want to turn my behavior around.
Don't want to become a criminal in this or any town.
Please listen to me and try to understand,
I'm still a young boy and not yet a man.
Sometimes I act before I think.
Maybe my brain is a bit out of sync.

~~~~~~~~~~~~~~~~~~

Again I say,
Don't Hate Me – Please Help Me

~~~~~~~~~~~~~~~~~~

"Feelings Do Matter"

How we feel affects our behavior.

When we feel better we behave better.

Education Is the Golden Key

I have heard some express concern
over why they should bother to learn.
There is not just one reason,
for learning has no one season.
Throughout the course of your life
application of what's been learned will minimize much strife.
For possessing useful knowledge leads to positive self-esteem.
Having this trait is much better than living in a bad dream.
To society you will be able to offer some needed useful skill.
You will not be counted among the lazy ones just sitting still.
Your educational process will reveal your hidden ability.
You will not appear to be suffering from senility.
With a good education you will experience upward mobility.
There will be no need to suffer from lack of mental agility.
Getting an education is the best way to occupy your time.
This leaves no openings for drugs that could blow your mind.
The only "crack" in your life is when you crack the books.
You should continue to study, no matter how it looks.
There will be those who will just try to barely get by.
They will never experience being on a natural high.
Learning is addictive when you apply yourself.
It will make life better than damaging stuff on the shelf.
Education helps to avoid the "Application Jitters".
It helps to avoid the "Rejection Bitters".
You want to land the best job in a unique space.
You must avoid the strain of an uphill race.
No need to live life looking for another to blame.
Without a good education you will live in shame.
You must decide who will benefit the most.
The benefactor should not be a "Ghost".
Look in the mirror and say, "I am learning for me".
"I'm honestly convinced that **Education Is the Golden Key**".

Feelings Do Matter .....Owl Letha's Messages to the Teens

1. Do not envy others, because things may not be as good as they look

2. Look in the mirror and love and respect the person that you see

3. Know that you have the ability and the power to get over most obstacles

4. Find at least one thing to be happy about everyday

5. Treat every challenge as an opportunity to grow and learn

6. Practice expressing appreciation for others and good things will come to you

7. Time is moving and you must make the most of every moment

8. You must wisely work to achieve what you expect to receive

9. When bad things happen, look at any possible lessons to be learned

10. A "Lazy mind" will hinder any personal progress

11. If you can't change something, it may be necessary to change your expectations

12. Continue to express love and tolerance and never spread hate

13. You are and will continue to be "A work in progress". So, continue the work

14. Live with an attitude of positivity and you live your life for the better

15. Never think of "work" as a bad word or a bad habit

16. Every day is a personal gift and should be gently unwrapped

17. There will be storms in life and you must prepare to weather each one

18. Life is complicated and you must seek others to help you during any difficulties

19. Inspire others who are doing good and you just might reap great benefits

20. Don't let your uncomfortable emotions get the best of you

21. Learn from the past and keep on moving towards a greater future

Feelings Do Matter …..Owl Letha's Messages to the Teens
(Continued)

22. See how the trees lose their leaves that turn brown but they keep on living

23. Time heals almost everything. So, give unpleasant things needed time to heal

24. You must remain the chief person who is in charge of your life and well-being

25. Remember that you are not alone with problems that need solving

26. Rely on those who have weathered many of life's challenges for valuable info

27. Growth can be painful but staying static can be emotionally draining

28. No one person knows everything. So, connect with a variety of well-versed people

29. When needing answers to life's problems, remember to visit the "Zone of Discovery"

30. One day please lovingly share your personal "Survival Guide"

www.ingramcontent.com/pod-product-compliance
Lightning Source LLC
Chambersburg PA
CBHW041214270326
41930CB00001B/13